Me 'n' Me

by
Beverly
Dyson
Crespo

illustrated by
Chris
Acemandese
Hall

First edition   10 9 8 7 6 5 4 3 2 1   Printed and bound in the United States of America

Library of Congress Cataloging-in-Publications Data
Crespo, Beverly, 1949-
    Melanin 'n' me/Beverly Crespo; illustrated by Chris Hall,
            p.   cm.
    Summary: Points out all the advantages of having melanin in the skin
                ISBN 1-463703-06-6
    [1. Melanin--Fiction.   2. Afro-Americans--Fiction.
        3. Stories in rhyme.]   I. Title.
        pz8.3.c866Me   1996
        [E]--dc20   96-3487

To Edward and Virginia Dyson
B. D. C.

I read a book the other day

About a chemical in our bodies
that colors the skin

The name of that chemical is melanin

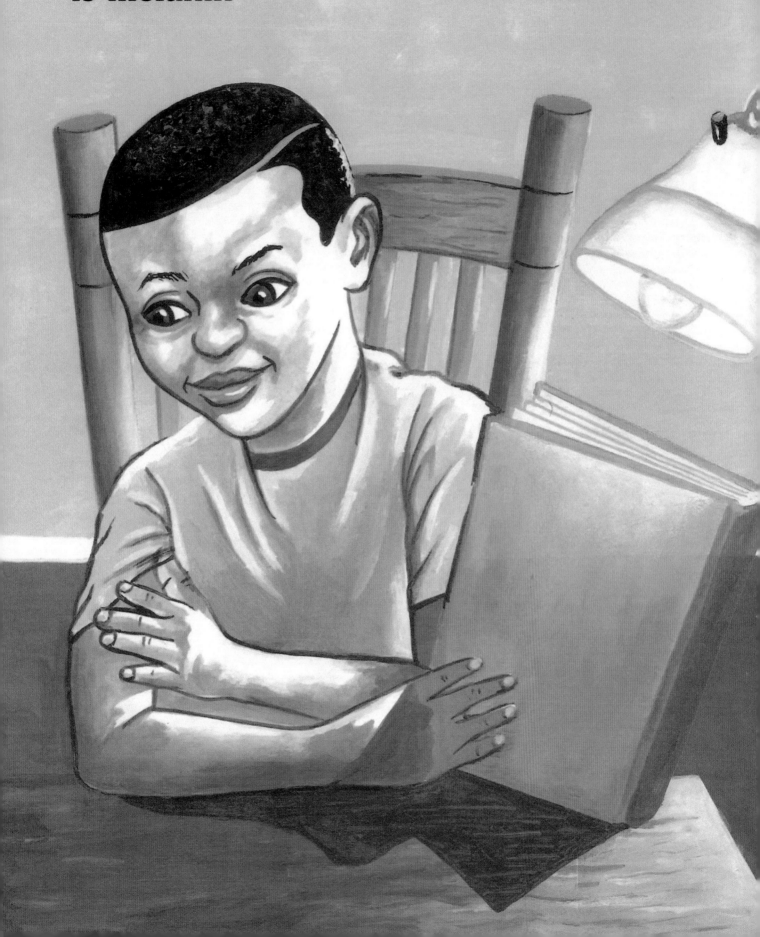

And I'm so glad it
put the brown in me.

It's even in my eyes
to help me see.

**Without it,
I could never play
beneath the sun**

Because harmful rays
could burn my skin
And ruin all the fun.

And my brothers and sisters are just like me.
They'd rather be in the sunshine,
not under a tree.

I asked my mother
what else melanin could do,

and she said,
"Honey, it
protects you
from diseases
too."

The next day
I raced to school
to tell my teacher all I knew.

She smiled at me and said, "Everything you say is true."

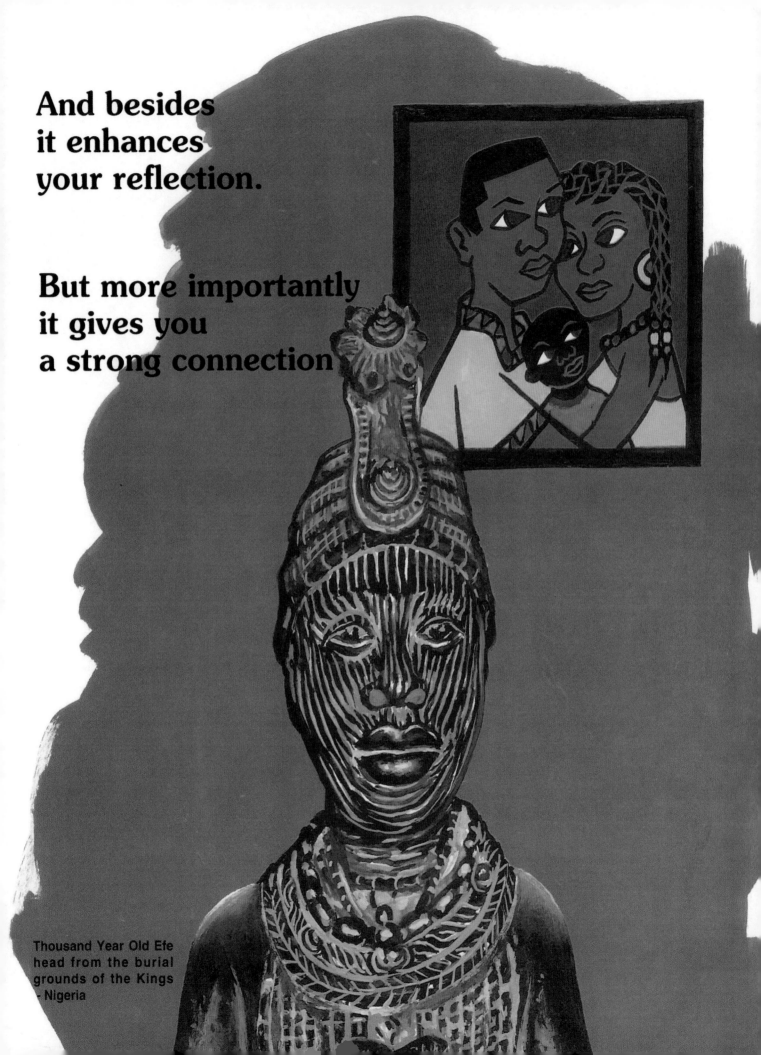

And besides
it enhances
your reflection.

But more importantly
it gives you
a strong connection

Thousand Year Old Efe
head from the burial
grounds of the Kings
- Nigeria

Well, for the rest of the day
I couldn't do a thing.

I just waited and waited
for that school bell to ring.

And when I got home,
I bent my knees to pray

And told God that
I would thank him
every day.

For having the wisdom
and foresight to see

How important it was
to put the melanin in me.

Melanin & Me

I read a book the other day
About a chemical in our bodies
that colors the skin
The name of that chemical is melanin
And I'm so glad it put the brown in me.
It's even in my eyes to help me see.

Without it, I could never play beneath the sun
Because harmful rays could burn my skin
And ruin all the fun.

Now, don't get me wrong I like shade.
Shade's okay.
But I wouldn't want to play, in it every day.
And my brothers and sisters are just like me.
They'd rather be in the sunshine,
not under a tree.

I asked my mother what else melanin could do,
and she said,
"Honey, it protects you from diseases too."

The next day I raced to school
to tell my teacher all I knew.
She smiled at me and said,
"Everything you say is true.
And besides it enhances your reflection.
But more importantly
it gives you a strong connection
to all of your relatives here and across the sea"

Well, for the rest of the day I couldn't do a
thing.
I just waited and waited
for that school bell to ring.
And when I got home, I bent my knees to pray
And told God that I would thank him every day
For having the wisdom and foresight to see
How important it was to put the melanin in me.

Beverly Crespo

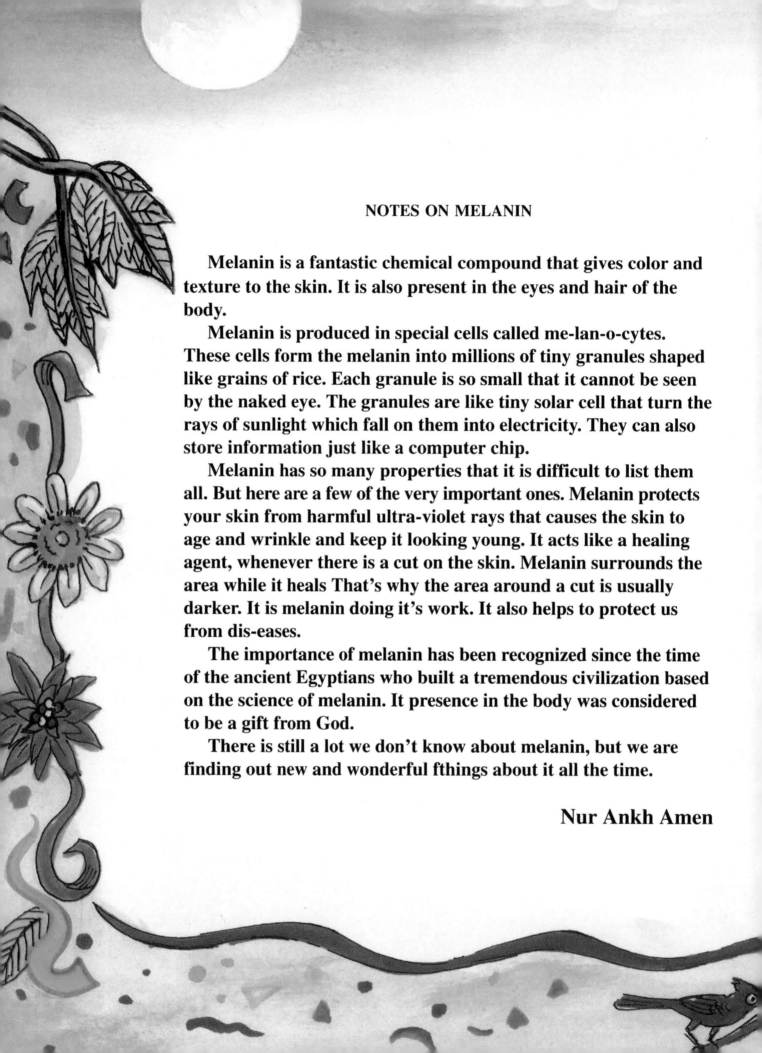

NOTES ON MELANIN

Melanin is a fantastic chemical compound that gives color and texture to the skin. It is also present in the eyes and hair of the body.

Melanin is produced in special cells called me-lan-o-cytes. These cells form the melanin into millions of tiny granules shaped like grains of rice. Each granule is so small that it cannot be seen by the naked eye. The granules are like tiny solar cell that turn the rays of sunlight which fall on them into electricity. They can also store information just like a computer chip.

Melanin has so many properties that it is difficult to list them all. But here are a few of the very important ones. Melanin protects your skin from harmful ultra-violet rays that causes the skin to age and wrinkle and keep it looking young. It acts like a healing agent, whenever there is a cut on the skin. Melanin surrounds the area while it heals That's why the area around a cut is usually darker. It is melanin doing it's work. It also helps to protect us from dis-eases.

The importance of melanin has been recognized since the time of the ancient Egyptians who built a tremendous civilization based on the science of melanin. It presence in the body was considered to be a gift from God.

There is still a lot we don't know about melanin, but we are finding out new and wonderful fthings about it all the time.

Nur Ankh Amen

HISTORY & CULTURE FOR YOUNG PEOPLE

Little Zeng's Abc's

by Chris Acemandese Hall

Made in the USA
Lexington, KY
28 June 2016